POMEGRANATE

POMEGRANATE

A BOOK OF RECIPES

HELEN SUDELL

LORENZ BOOKS

First published in 2015 by Lorenz Books
an imprint of Anness Publishing Limited
108 Great Russell Street, London WC1B 3NA
www.annesspublishing.com
www.lorenzbooks.com; info@anness.com

If you like the images in this book and would like to investigate
using them for publishing, promotions or advertising, please visit
our website www.practicalpictures.com for more information

A CIP catalogue record for this book is available from
The British Library

Publisher: Joanna Lorenz
Editorial Director: Helen Sudell
Designer: Nigel Partridge
Illustrations: Anna Koska
Production Controller: Pirong Wang

Photographers: Martin Brigdale, Nicki Dowey, William Lingwood,
Jon Whitaker, Gus Filgate

Printed and bound in China

PUBLISHER'S NOTE

Although the advice and information in this book are believed to
be accurate and true at the time of going to press, neither the
authors nor the publisher can accept any legal responsibility or
liability for any errors or omissions that may have been made nor
for any inaccuracies nor for any loss, harm or injury that comes
about from following instructions or advice in this book.

COOK'S NOTES

· Bracketed terms are intended for American readers.

· For all recipes, quantities are given in both metric and imperial
measures and, where appropriate, in standard cups and spoons.
Follow one set of measures, but not a mixture, because they are
not interchangeable.

· Standard spoon and cup measures are level. 1 tsp = 5ml,
1 tbsp = 15ml, 1 cup = 250ml/8fl oz.

· Australian standard tablespoons are 20ml. Australian readers
should use 3 tsp in place of 1 tbsp for measuring small quantities.

· American pints are 16fl oz/2 cups. American readers should use
20fl oz/2.5 cups in place of 1 pint when measuring liquids.

· Electric oven temperatures in this book are for conventional
ovens. When using a fan oven, the temperature will probably need
to be reduced by about 10–20°C/20–40°F. Since ovens vary, you
should check with your manufacturer's instruction book for
guidance.

· The nutritional analysis given for each recipe is calculated per
portion (i.e. serving or item), unless otherwise stated. If the recipe
gives a range, such as Serves 4–6, then the nutritional analysis will
be for the smaller portion size, i.e. 6 servings. The analysis does not
include optional ingredients, such as salt added to taste.

· Medium (US large) eggs are used unless otherwise stated.

· If you prefer to buy fresh pomegranate seeds from a specialist
food store or middle-eastern delicatessen, bear in mind that the
average ripe pomegranate weighs around 250g/9oz and will yield
165g/5½oz/1 cup pomegranate seeds.

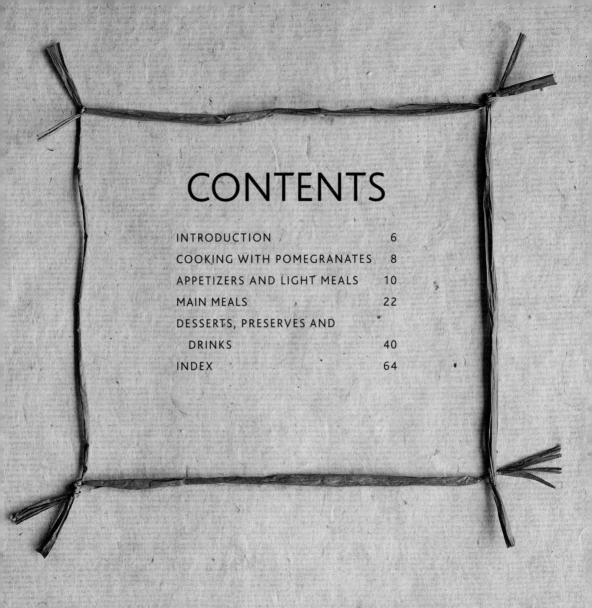

CONTENTS

INTRODUCTION

This attractive, apple-shaped fruit has leathery reddish-gold skin and a large calyx or crown. Inside is a mass of creamy edible seeds, each encased in a translucent sac of deep pink or crimson pulp and held together by segments of bitter, inedible, yellow membrane that extend outwards to the skin. These seeds gave the fruit its name, which means 'grain apple'.

Eating a pomegranate is quite hard work, as each fleshy seed must be picked out individually,

Below: Pomegranates are bright red when ripe.

but their delicate, slightly tart flavour and refreshing, juicy texture make the effort worthwhile. Be warned, however, that pomegranate juice stains indelibly.

HISTORY

Originally from Persia, pomegranates have been linked with many cultures and religions for centuries, and have been a symbol of fertility since ancient times because of their numerous seeds. The goddess Aphrodite is said to have planted a pomegranate tree in her birthplace in Cyprus, and the Romans, who referred to the fruit as the 'apple of Carthage', consumed it in vast quantities and made wine from the fermented juice. In medieval times, Islamic mystics believed pomegranates could elevate the soul and purge it of hate, anger and envy.

Both sweet and sour pomegranates were cultivated

Above: Pomegranates are referred to in the Qur'an as the fruit of paradise.

during the Ottoman period. The sour variety was valued for its juice, which was used to make a refreshing drink, and as a souring agent before the arrival of lemons in the region.

COOKING

Pomegranate juice is delicious in refreshing long drinks, such as pomegranate-flavoured lemonade, or it can be used to make a syrup to colour and flavour drinks and cocktails. The juice can also be used for sorbets and sauces, and makes a delicious pink jelly for savoury dishes. The juice is also used to prepare a special molasses, which is sour to taste and is used for dressing salads or as a marinade for poultry.

Below: Pomegranate seeds are encased in a deep pink pulp.

The jewel-like seeds of the sweet pomegranate can be sprinkled with a little rose water and served as a dessert, and they are also added to both savoury and sweet dishes as a colourful garnish.

HEALTH BENEFITS

The juice of the pomegranate is an excellent source of Vitamin C. However, it is the antioxidant polyphenol content contained within the juice that is thought to be responsible for some of its more far-reaching health benefits. Mainly in the realm of heart health, these polyphenols can reduce risk factors such as atherosclerosis and blood pressure as they are able to protect cells from oxidative stress. Pomegranate juice may also have anti-viral and anti-bacterial properties, especially in the mouth, and may protect against tooth decay.

The seeds are packed full of vitamin C and are a good source of dietary fibre. Since high-fibre foods keep the body satisfied for longer, eating pomegranate seeds can help reduce weight loss. They are easy to incorporate into your diet: sprinkle them on porridge or Greek yogurt for breakfast; add to a fresh green salad at lunchtime, and spread across roasted vegetables such as carrots or brussels sprouts.

Below: Pomegranate juice is full of heart-healthy polyphenols.

COOKING WITH POMEGRANATES

When buying pomegranates choose glossy fruit and avoid those whose skin looks hard and dry. Pomegranates that feel heavy for their size are likely to be full of juice.

PREPARING POMEGRANATES

1 Wash the fruit then cut off a thin slice from one end.

2 Stand the fruit upright. Cut downwards through the skin at intervals, using a sharp knife.

3 Bend back the segments and use your fingers to push the seeds into a bowl.

4 Remove all the bitter white pith and membrane. Give yourself a treat by sampling a selection of the seeds.

EXTRACTING THE JUICE

Although you can buy pomegranate juice you can also extract your own.

Heat the fruit for 30 seconds on high in a microwave, then roll gently on the work surface to burst the seeds. Make a hole in the bottom, stand over a small bowl and let the juice drain out, squeezing the pomegranate occasionally.

Alternatively, put the seeds in a strainer set over a bowl and crush gently. Do not try to extract the juice with electric juicers as they will crush the seeds and make the juice bitter.

POMEGRANATE AND SUMAC SALAD DRESSING
This Lebanese dressing will enliven any salad.

Whisk together 30ml/ 2 tbsp olive oil with 30ml/2 tbsp pomegranate syrup and 5–10ml1–2 tsp ground sumac.

Pour the dressing over a salad made up of leafy greens, or shredded vegetables, and toss just before serving.

MEDIEVAL POMEGRANATE SAUCE

This sauce works well as a marinade or as a dressing for poultry and game birds.

Using a mortar and pestle, crush and grind 2 cloves of garlic with 5ml/1 tsp salt to a smooth paste.

In a bowl, combine the creamed garlic with 30ml/2 tbsp olive oil and 60ml/4 tbsp pomegranate molasses.

Add a small bunch of fresh mint leaves, finely chopped, and 5–10ml/1–2 tsp ground sumac. Use as a marinade before cooking, or serve with grilled (broiled) or roast chicken or game.

POMEGRANATE CUCUMBER SALAD

This simple Persian recipe is delicious served as part of a mezze or as an accompaniment to grilled meats.

Cut 2 fresh pomegranates into quarters and take out the seeds, discarding any white pith. Cut 1 peeled cucumber in half lengthways and slice it finely. Cut 1 peeled red onion in half lengthways, then in half crossways, and slice it with the grain. Mix the sliced vegetables with a small bunch of shredded frest mint leaves and stir to mix. Toss the ingredients in lemon juice, season and serve.

MAKING POMEGRANATE MOLASSES

This syrup is used in salad dressings and marinades, and is often drizzled over dishes to add its exquisite fruity, sour note.

In a pan, heat 1 litre/32fl oz/ 4 cups pomegranate juice, 125g/4oz/½ cup sugar and 50ml/2fl oz/¼ cup lemon juice on medium high until the sugar has dissolved. Simmer for about an hour, until the juice has a syrup consistency and has reduced to 250ml/8fl oz/ 1 cup. Pour into a sterilized jar, allow to cool and store in the refrigerator.

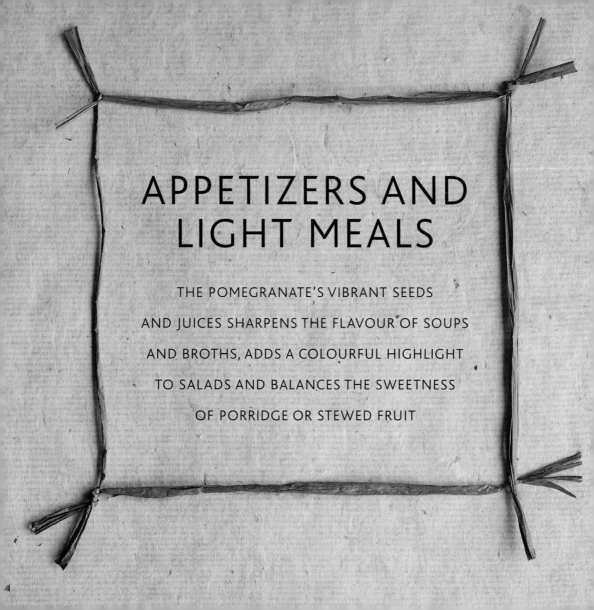

APPETIZERS AND LIGHT MEALS

THE POMEGRANATE'S VIBRANT SEEDS
AND JUICES SHARPENS THE FLAVOUR OF SOUPS
AND BROTHS, ADDS A COLOURFUL HIGHLIGHT
TO SALADS AND BALANCES THE SWEETNESS
OF PORRIDGE OR STEWED FRUIT

POMEGRANATE BROTH

With its origins in Persia and Azerbaijan, this fresh-tasting delicate soup, narlı çorba, *is perhaps the best way of appreciating sour pomegranates, as it is both pleasing to the eye and the palate.*

Serves 4

1.2 litres/2 pints/5 cups clear chicken stock
150ml/¼ pint/⅔ cup pomegranate juice, sour if possible, sweet if not (to make your own juice see page 8)
juice of 1 lemon (optional)
seeds of 1 sweet pomegranate
salt and ground black pepper
fresh mint leaves, to garnish

> **COOK'S TIP**
> Sour pomegranates are available in Middle Eastern stores, but if you can only find sweet pomegranates, use them with the juice of a lemon.

Energy 62kcal/260kJ; Protein 2g; Carbohydrate 3.9g, of which sugars 2.3g; Fat 4.4g, of which saturates 0.4g; Cholesterol 0mg; Calcium 14mg; Fibre 0.6g; Sodium 205mg.

Pour the stock into a pan and bring to the boil. Lower the heat, stir in the pomegranate juice, and lemon juice if using sweet pomegranate juice, then bring the stock back to the boil.

Lower the heat again and stir in half the pomegranate seeds, then season and turn off the heat.

Ladle the hot broth into warmed bowls. Sprinkle the remaining pomegranate seeds over the top and garnish with mint leaves.

CHICKEN SOUP WITH ONIONS AND POMEGRANATE SEEDS

This dish could be described as a Middle Eastern 'Coq au Vin' as it is half soup, half stew. The pomegranate seeds add a rich ruby colour to the soup.

Serves 4

For the marinated onions
2 onions, halved and sliced
seeds of half a pomegranate
30ml/2 tbsp white wine vinegar

For serving
225g/8oz dried melokhia
    (mallow) leaves
1 chicken, approximately
    1kg/2lb in weight
1.2 litres/2 pints/5 cups water
2 onions, quartered
2 carrots, peeled and each cut
    into 3
2 cloves garlic, smashed in their
    skins
4–5 cloves
3–4 cardamom pods
crusty bread, to serve
sea salt and ground black
    pepper

Energy 342kcal/1441kJ; Protein 50g;
Carbohydrate 21g, of which sugars 16g; Fat
7g, of which saturates 2g; Cholesterol
180mg; Calcium 133mg; Fibre 6.3g;
Sodium 276mg.

Place the onions and pomegranate seeds in a bowl and toss in the vinegar. Cover and set aside to marinate.

Crush the dried melokhia leaves with your hand and place them in a bowl. Pour over just enough boiling water to cover and leave them to soak until they have doubled in bulk.

Place the chicken in a deep pot and cover with the water. Add the onions, carrots, garlic, cloves, cardamom pods and seasoning.

Bring the water in the pot to the boil then reduce the heat, cover, and simmer for about 25 minutes. Stir in the melokhia leaves and simmer, uncovered, for a further 25 minutes.

Lift the chicken out of the pot and check the seasoning of the stock. If it lacks flavour, boil rapidly for 10 minutes to reduce. Skin the chicken, cut it into joints, and return to the stock.

Serve the chicken in shallow bowls, spooning the carrots and melokhia leaves over it. Top each bowl with a spoonful of the marinated onions and pomegranate seeds, and serve with plenty of bread.

POMEGRANATE AND MOLASSES PORRIDGE

Vibrant pink pomegranate – rich in fibre, potassium and vitamin C – looks wonderful stirred into this caramel-coloured porridge and is the perfect healthy start to the day.

Serves 4
125g/4¼oz/¾ cup quinoa
250ml/8fl oz/1 cup boiling water
300ml/½ pint/1¼ cups milk
60ml/4 tbsp molasses syrup
clear honey, to taste
seeds of 1 pomegranate

Put the quinoa in a sieve (strainer) and rinse under cold running water.

Transfer the rinsed quinoa to a pan, then add the boiling water and milk. You can use cold water instead of boiling water, if you prefer, but the quinoa will take longer to cook.

Simmer the quinoa for 15 minutes, until soft. Stir in the molasses and sweeten with honey as required.

Remove from the heat and stir in the pomegranate seeds. Serve drizzled with a little more honey, if you wish.

Gluten Free: Energy 238kcal/1002kJ; Protein 7g; Carbohydrate 44g, of which sugars 24g; Fat 5g, of which saturates 2g; Cholesterol 10mg; Calcium 144mg; Fibre 2g; Sodium 44mg.

COOK'S TIP
Molasses syrup, a by-product of sugar production, provides precious calcium and iron, but may need sweetening with a drizzle of honey.

STUFFED PRUNES IN A POMEGRANATE SAUCE

In Armenian cuisine, prunes, apricots and figs are often stuffed with nuts or with an aromatic rice mixture. This delicious dish of prunes in a spicy pomegranate sauce makes an unusual mezze dish.

Serves 4

12–16 ready-to-eat, pitted prunes
12–16 walnut halves
15–30ml/1-2 tbsp ghee or olive oil with a knob (pat) of butter
30–45ml/2–3 tbsp pomegranate molasses
30ml/2 tbsp sugar
1 cinnamon stick
3–4 cardamom pods
2–3 cloves
juice of 1 lemon
250ml/9fl oz red wine or water
sea salt and ground black pepper
1 small bunch flat leaf parsley, chopped

Find the opening in each pitted prune and stuff it with a walnut half.

Melt the ghee, or olive oil and butter, in a heavy pan and toss in the prunes for 2-3 minutes, turning them over from time to time. Stir in the pomegranate molasses with the sugar and spices, and add the lemon juice and wine and water.

Season with salt and pepper and bring the liquid to the boil. Reduce the heat and simmer, uncovered, for about 15 minutes, stirring occasionally, until the prunes are tender.

Arrange the prunes on a serving dish and spoon the pomegranate sauce over and around them. Garnish with the parsley and serve hot or at room temperature.

Energy 244kcal/1021kJ; Protein 1g; Carbohydrate 34g, of which sugars 32g; Fat 8g, of which saturates 5g; Cholesterol 21mg; Calcium 72mg; Fibre 2.7g; Sodium 116mg.

MUHAMMARA

This spicy walnut and pomegranate dip is delicious served as a mezze dish. The labneh needs to be prepared 48 hours ahead, or you can buy ready prepared labneh in Middle Eastern stores.

Serves 6
For the labneh
450g/1lb Greek (US strained plain) yogurt
2.5ml/½ tsp sea salt

For the muhammara
2 red (bell) peppers
1 red chilli, seeded and finely chopped
2 cloves garlic, crushed with sea salt
125g/4½oz walnuts, roughly chopped
30–45ml/2–3 tbsp toasted breadcrumbs
15ml/1 tbsp pomegranate molasses
juice of ½ a lemon
5ml/1 tsp sugar
45ml/3 tbsp olive oil
sea salt

Energy 319kcal/1327kJ; Protein 9g; Carbohydrate 17g, of which sugars 13g; Fat 24g, of which saturates 4g; Cholesterol 8mg; Calcium 188mg; Fibre 1.8 g; Sodium 332mg.

To prepare the labneh, beat the yogurt with the salt and tip it into a piece of muslin (cheesecloth) lining a colander.

Pull up the four corners of the muslin, tie them together and suspend the bundle from the handle of a wooden spoon placed over a deep bowl, a bucket, or the sink.

Leave the yogurt to drain in a cool place for at least 48 hours. Pour off the whey that collects in the bowl as necessary.

When the yogurt has reduced to half the original amount (roughly 225g/8oz) and is the consistency of cream cheese, transfer to a large, clean bowl.

To prepare the muhammara, place the peppers directly over a gas flame, or over a charcoal grill, and roast them until the skin is charred and buckled.

Place the peppers in a plastic bag to sweat for 5 minutes and loosen the skins. Remove from the bag, peel off the skins and remove the stalks and seeds. Chop the pepper flesh into very small pieces.

Using a mortar and pestle, pound the chopped peppers with chopped chilli, garlic, and walnuts to a fairly smooth paste. You could use a food processor for this, but pulse rather than blend for a rough, chopped consistency.

Beat the breadcrumbs, the pomegranate molasses, lemon juice and the sugar into the pepper and walnut paste.

Drizzle the oil into the mixture, beating all the time, until the consistency is thick and creamy.

Add the muhammara to the bowl of labneh and combine. Check the seasoning, drizzle a little olive oil over the top and serve with sticks of carrot, celery, bell pepper and spring onions (scallions).

AUBERGINE WITH POMEGRANATE SEEDS

A favourite dish throughout the eastern Mediterranean, serve it warm or at room temperature to make the most of the smoky flavour of the aubergine and the sharp crunch of the pomegranate seeds.

Serves 4–6

2 aubergines (eggplants)
2 tomatoes, skinned, seeded and chopped
1 green (bell) pepper, chopped
1 red onion, finely chopped
1 bunch flat leaf parsley, finely chopped
2 cloves garlic, crushed
30–45ml/2–3 tbsp olive oil
juice of 1 lemon
15–30ml/1–2 tbsp walnuts, finely chopped
15–30ml/1–2 tbsp pomegranate seeds, plus wedges, to serve
sea salt and ground black pepper

Place the aubergines on a hot griddle, or directly over a gas flame, and leave to char until soft, turning occasionally.

Hold the aubergines by their stems under running cold water and peel off the charred skins, or slit open the skins and scoop out the flesh.

Squeeze out the excess water from the aubergine flesh then chop it to a pulp and place it in a bowl with the tomatoes, pepper, onion, parsley and garlic. Add the olive oil and lemon juice and toss thoroughly. Season to taste with salt and pepper, then stir in half the walnuts and pomegranate seeds.

Turn the salad into a serving dish and garnish with the remaining walnuts and pomegranate wedges.

Energy 90kcal/374kJ; Protein 2.2g; Carbohydrate 7.3g, of which sugars 6.3g; Fat 6g, of which saturates 0.8g; Cholesterol 0mg; Calcium 39mg; Fibre 3.1g; Sodium 10mg.

MAIN MEALS

WHETHER ADDED TO MARINADES, OR SIMPLY
SPRINKLED OVER GRILLED FISH, POMEGRANATE
LENDS A PIQUANT FRESHNESS TO A WIDE RANGE OF
MAIN DISHES. POMEGRANATE ALSO COMBINES
BEAUTIFULLY WITH POULTRY AND CUTS THROUGH
THE RICHNESS OF GAME BIRDS. VEGETABLES ARE
EQUALLY ENHANCED BY THESE BRIGHT JEWELS

FISH WITH TOMATO AND POMEGRANATE SAUCE

This is a tasty method of cooking any firm-fleshed fish, such as sea bass, red snapper, grouper and trout. The pomegranate molasses adds a tangy, sour note to the sauce and enriches the colour.

Serves 4

900g/2lb firm-fleshed fish fillets
45–60ml/3–4 tbsp olive oil
juice of 1 lemon
2–3 cloves garlic, finely chopped
4 tomatoes, skinned, seeded, and chopped
15ml/1 tbsp pomegranate molasses
10ml/2 tsp sugar
salt and ground black pepper
1 small bunch fresh parsley, finely chopped, to garnish

Energy 284kcal/1192kJ; Protein 41.7g;
Carbohydrate 6.9g, of which sugars 6.9g;
Fat 10.1g, of which saturates 1.5g;
Cholesterol 104mg; Calcium 28mg; Fibre
0.8g; Sodium 149mg.

Preheat the oven to 180°C/350°F/Gas 4. Arrange the fish in an ovenproof dish, and rub with salt and pepper.

Pour 30ml/2 tbsp olive oil and the lemon juice over the fish. Cover with foil and bake for about 25 minutes, until the fish is cooked.

Meanwhile, heat the rest of the oil in a heavy frying pan. Fry the garlic until it begins to colour, then add the tomatoes. Cook for 5 minutes, then stir in the pomegranate molasses with the sugar. Reduce the heat and cook gently until the sauce thickens. Season with salt and pepper. Keep warm.

Arrange the fish on a serving dish, spoon the sauce over and around the fish and sprinkle with the parsley.

SINIYA

The name of this Sephardi dish means fish and tahini sauce. The fish is wrapped in vine leaves, then spread with tahini and baked. A sprinkling of pomegranate seeds adds a fresh, invigorating flavour.

Serves 4

4 small fish, such as trout, sea bream or red mullet, each weighing about 300g/11oz, cleaned
at least 5 garlic cloves, chopped
juice of 2 lemons
75ml/5 tbsp olive oil
about 20 brined vine leaves
tahini, for drizzling
1–2 pomegranates
fresh mint and coriander (cilantro) sprigs, to garnish

VARIATION

Instead of whole fish, use fish fillets or steaks such as fresh tuna. Make a bed of vine leaves and top with the fish and marinade. Bake for 5–10 minutes until the fish is half cooked, then top with the tahini as above and grill (broil) until golden brown and lightly crusted.

Preheat the oven to 180°C/350°F/Gas 4. Put the fish in a shallow, ovenproof dish, large enough to fit the whole fish without touching each other. In a bowl, combine the garlic, lemon juice and oil; spoon over the fish. Turn the fish to coat.

Rinse the vine leaves well under cold water, then wrap the fish in the leaves. Arrange the fish in the same dish and spoon any marinade in the dish over the top of each. Bake for 30 minutes.

Drizzle the tahini over the top of each wrapped fish, making a ribbon so that the tops and tails of the fish and some of the vine leaf wrapping still show. Return to the oven and bake for a further 5–10 minutes until the top is golden and slightly crusted.

Meanwhile, cut the pomegranates in half and scoop out the seeds. Sprinkle the seeds over the fish, garnish with sprigs of mint and coriander, and serve.

Energy 402kcal/1681kJ; Protein 46.8g; Carbohydrate 2.6g, of which sugars 2.6g; Fat 22.8g, of which saturates 4.1g; Cholesterol 192mg; Calcium 86mg; Fibre 0.5g; Sodium 176mg.

ROASTED FISH WITH CHILLIES AND WALNUTS

This is a classic Lebanese meal that is great with any type of firm-fleshed fish. Topped with a spicy tahini sauce, this dish is spectacular when garnished with jewel-like fresh pomegranate seeds.

Serves 4

2 x 900g/2lb firm-fleshed fish, gutted and cleaned
60ml/4 tbsp olive oil
2 onions, finely chopped
1 green (bell) pepper, very finely chopped
1–2 red chillies, seeded and very finely chopped
115g/4oz walnuts, chopped
15–30ml/1–2 tbsp pomegranate molasses
small bunches of fresh coriander (cilantro) and flat leaf parsley, finely chopped
salt and ground black pepper

For the sauce

15ml/1 tbsp olive oil
2 cloves garlic, finely chopped
1–2 red chillies, seeded and finely chopped
60ml/4 tbsp tahini
juice of 1 lemon
juice of 1 orange
salt and ground black pepper
seeds of ½ pomegranate

Preheat the oven to 200°C/400°F/Gas 6. With a sharp knife, make three or four diagonal slits on each side of the fish. Rub the cavity with salt and pepper, cover and chill for 30 minutes.

Meanwhile, prepare the filling. Heat 30ml/2 tbsp olive oil in a heavy pan and fry the onions, pepper and chillies until lightly browned. Stir in the walnuts and pomegranate molasses, and add half the fresh coriander and parsley. Season to taste and leave the filling to cool.

Fill the fish with the stuffing and secure the opening with a wooden skewer or cocktail sticks (toothpicks).

Place the fish in an oiled baking dish and pour over the remaining oil. Bake in the preheated oven for about 30 minutes.

For the tahini sauce, heat the olive oil in a small pan and stir in the garlic and chillies, until they begin to colour.

In a bowl, beat the tahini with the lemon and orange juice, until the mixture is smooth and creamy. Add the garlic and chilli mixture, beat to mix, then return to the pan and warm the sauce through. Season with salt and pepper and keep warm.

Transfer the cooked fish to a serving dish and drizzle some of the sauce over the top. Garnish with the pomegranate seeds and serve immediately, with the rest of the sauce served separately.

Energy 772kcal/3223kJ; Protein 78.8g; Carbohydrate 13.1g, of which sugars 10.3g; Fat 45.3g, of which saturates 6.5g; Cholesterol 288mg; Calcium 292mg; Fibre 4.9g; Sodium 276mg.

SAUTÉED LIVER WITH POMEGRANATE SYRUP

Lamb's or calf's liver is very tender and makes a deliciously different main course. Sautéed or grilled, it is mixed with pomegranate syrup which gives it a distinctive dark rich colouring.

Serves 4

30ml/2 tbsp olive oil
2 red onions, halved and thinly
    sliced
2–3 cloves garlic, finely
    chopped
450g/1lb lamb's liver, cut into
    bite size pieces
5ml/1 tsp ground cinnamon
2.5ml/½ tsp ground allspice
sea salt and ground black
    pepper
juice of 1 lemon
5–10ml/1–2 tsp pomegranate
    syrup

Heat the oil in a heavy-based pan and stir in the sliced onions and garlic. Once the onions begin to colour, toss in the liver for 2-3 minutes, until browned.

Stir in the spices and seasoning and add the lemon juice. Drizzle the pomegranate syrup over the liver and serve immediately from the pan.

Energy 257kcal/1074kJ; Protein 24g; Carbohydrate 8g, of which sugars 6g; Fat 15g, of which saturates 3g; Cholesterol 484mg; Calcium 46mg; Fibre 1.2g; Sodium 185mg.

COOK'S TIP
Pomegranate syrup, also sold as pomegranate molasses, is available from Middle Eastern stores and some delicatessens.

CHICKEN WITH WALNUTS AND POMEGRANATE JUICE

This delicious stew brings together the classic combination of walnuts and pomegranates to create a warming, comforting family dish. Serve with a plain pilaff and a leafy salad.

Serves 4

3 pomegranates
juice of 1 lemon
30ml/2 tbsp ghee or butter
2 onions, finely chopped
1 medium chicken, jointed
5–10ml/1–2 tsp ground
   cinnamon
5ml/1 tsp sugar
225g/8oz/1⅓ cup walnuts,
   crushed
salt and ground black pepper
a few shredded mint leaves,
   to garnish

Halve the pomegranates. Extract the seeds from one of the halves and set them aside for the garnish. Squeeze the remaining pomegranate halves over a bowl to extract the juice. Add the lemon juice and mix together well.

Melt the ghee or butter in a heavy pan or flameproof casserole. Stir in the onions and fry until they begin to colour. Add the chicken joints to the pan and brown them lightly.

Pour over the pomegranate and lemon juice and stir in the cinnamon and sugar. Season with salt and pepper.

Bring the liquid to a gentle boil, then turn down the heat. Cover the pan and simmer for about 35 minutes – top up the liquid with a little water if the mixture becomes dry.

Meanwhile, heat the oven to 200°C/400°F/Gas 6. Transfer to an ovenproof dish or remove the lid from the casserole, and sprinkle the walnuts over the chicken. Place in the oven and roast the walnuts on top of the chicken for about 10 minutes, or until the walnuts become golden.

Transfer the chicken pieces to a serving dish. Stir the walnuts into the remaining juice in the pan and spoon them over and around the chicken. Sprinkle the reserved pomegranate seeds over the top and garnish with the shredded mint.

Energy 867kcal/3591kJ; Protein 40.6g; Carbohydrate 17.4g, of which sugars 13.8g; Fat 71.1g, of which saturates 14.6g; Cholesterol 176mg; Calcium 99mg; Fibre 4.6g; Sodium 180mg.

CHARGRILLED QUAILS IN POMEGRANATE MARINADE

This is a simple and tasty way of serving small birds, such as quails, poussins or grouse. The sharp marinade tenderizes the meat, as well as enhancing its flavour.

Serves 4

*4 quails, cleaned and boned
  – ask your butcher to do this
juice of 4 pomegranates
juice of 1 lemon
30ml/2 tbsp olive oil
5–10ml/1–2 tsp Turkish red
  pepper, or 5ml/1 tsp chilli
  powder
30–45ml/2–3 tbsp thick and
  creamy natural (plain) yogurt
1 bunch of fresh flat leaf parsley
seeds of ½ pomegranate
salt*

Soak eight wooden skewers in hot water for about 15 minutes, then drain. Thread one skewer through the wings of each bird and a second skewer through the legs to keep them together.

Place the skewered birds in a wide, shallow dish. Beat the pomegranate and lemon juice with the oil and red pepper or chilli powder, pour over the quails and rub it into the skin. Cover with foil and leave to marinate in a cold place or the refrigerator for 2–3 hours, turning the birds over from time to time.

Get the barbecue ready for cooking. Lift the birds out of the marinade and pour what is left of it into a bowl. Beat the yogurt into the leftover marinade and add a little salt.

Brush some of the yogurt mixture over the birds and place them on the prepared barbecue.

Cook for 4–5 minutes on each side, brushing with the yogurt as they cook to form a crust.

Chop some of the parsley and lay the rest on a serving dish. Place the cooked quails on the parsley and sprinkle with the pomegranate seeds and the chopped parsley. Serve hot.

Energy 288kcal/1207kJ; Protein 37.4g; Carbohydrate 5.8g, of which sugars 5.8g; Fat 13g, of which saturates 2.7g; Cholesterol 0mg; Calcium 84mg; Fibre 0.5g; Sodium 111mg.

COOK'S TIP

Turkish red pepper is a common condiment in Syria and Turkey and is made from the crushed dried flakes of the Aleppo pepper. It is available from Middle Eastern stores and some delicatessens.

DUCK TAGINE WITH POMEGRANATE AND CHESTNUTS

*This is a lovely aromatic, winter dish, decorated with bright green fresh herbs and ruby-red
pomegranate seeds – ideal for seasonal celebrations.*

Serves 4

30ml/2 tbsp ghee
2 onions, finely chopped
4 garlic cloves, finely chopped
*25g/1oz fresh ginger, finely
chopped*
10ml/2 tsp cumin seeds
2–3 dried red chillies, left whole
4 duck legs
*600ml/1 pint/2½ cups chicken
stock*
300g/10oz shelled chestnuts
30ml/2 tbsp honey
salt and ground black pepper
seeds of 1 pomegranate
*a small bunch of fresh mint
leaves, finely chopped*
*a small bunch of fresh coriander
(cilantro), finely chopped*
couscous, to serve

Energy 614kcal/2575kJ; Protein 53.1g;
Carbohydrate 44.9g, of which sugars 19.9g;
Fat 26.6g, of which saturates 9.1g;
Cholesterol 275mg; Calcium 136mg; Fibre
7.7g; Sodium 295mg.

Heat the ghee in the base of a flameproof tagine or shallow heavy pan,
and stir in the onions, garlic, ginger and cumin seeds. Cook for 2–3
minutes, until they begin to colour.

Add the dried chillies and duck legs. Pour in the chicken stock and
bring it to the boil. Reduce the heat, cover with a lid, and simmer gently
for 25–30 minutes.

Add the chestnuts and honey, put the lid back on, and cook gently
for a further 25–30 minutes, until the chicken is very tender.

Season with salt and plenty of black pepper, and add most of the
pomegranate seeds, fresh mint and fresh coriander, reserving some for
the garnish. Cook for 5–10 minutes more.

Garnish with the reserved pomegranate seeds and herbs, and serve
the tagine with couscous.

FRIED VEGETABLES WITH POMEGRANATE SEEDS

This very simple, tasty dish combines fried aubergine, courgettes and peppers with a garlicky yogurt. The pomegranate adds colour as well as flavour.

Serves 4

1 large aubergine (eggplant)
1 courgette (zucchini)
1 red (bell) pepper
4 Turkish çarliston peppers,
  kept whole with stalk
sunflower oil, for deep-frying
200ml/7fl oz/scant 1 cup thick
  and creamy natural (plain)
  yogurt
2–3 garlic cloves, crushed
30–45ml/2–3 tbsp
  pomegranate seeds
salt and ground black pepper

Using a vegetable peeler, partially peel the aubergine in stripes.

Cut the aubergine in half lengthways and then cut each half into thick slices. Drop the slices into a bowl of salted water to prevent them discolouring. Drain and squeeze them dry before frying, otherwise the excess water will cause the hot oil to spatter everywhere.

Cut the courgette in half lengthways and then cut it widthways into thick slices. Deseed the red pepper and cut it into bitesize pieces.

Heat enough oil for deep-frying in a wide pan. Fry the vegetables in batches, until they are golden brown. Lift them out of the oil with tongs or a slotted spoon and drain on kitchen paper.

In a bowl, beat the yogurt with the garlic, and season to taste with salt and pepper. Pile the hot vegetables on to a serving dish and spoon the yogurt over the top, reserving 15–30ml/1–2 tbsp in the base of the bowl.

Fold half the pomegranate seeds into the remaining yogurt and spoon the mixture over the top of the prepared dish. Sprinkle with the remainder of the pomegranate seeds.

Serve immediately, while the vegetables are still warm, to contrast with the cool yogurt. Accompany with chunks of fresh, crusty bread to scoop and mop up the tasty sauce.

Energy 225kcal/933kJ; Protein 6.5g; Carbohydrate 13.3g, of which sugars 11.6g; Fat 17.1g, of which saturates 4.2g; Cholesterol 0mg; Calcium 104mg; Fibre 4g; Sodium 43mg.

COURGETTES WITH POMEGRANATE AND PINE NUTS

Creamy courgettes, stuffed with bright red pomegranate seeds and dry-roasted pine nuts, makes a satisfying summer meal. The feta cheese adds a delicious final tang to the dish.

Serves 4

115g/4oz/1 cup pine nuts
8 pale-green courgettes (zucchini)
30ml/2 tbsp olive oil, plus extra for drizzling
1 onion, finely chopped
2 garlic cloves, crushed
2.5ml/½ tsp ground allspice
2.5ml/½ tsp ground cinnamon
185g/6½oz/scant 1 cup long grain rice
seeds of 2 pomegranates
60ml/4 tbsp chopped fresh parsley
salt and ground black pepper
115g/4oz feta cheese, to serve

Energy 494kcal/2048kJ; Protein 12.4g;
Carbohydrate 51.1g, of which sugars 12g;
Fat 26.7g, of which saturates 2.3g;
Cholesterol 0mg; Calcium 109mg; Fibre 4g;
Sodium 10mg.

Put the pine nuts in a dry pan and toast over medium-high heat, tossing regularly, for 1–2 minutes, or until golden brown. Set aside. Halve the courgettes lengthways. Using a small sharp knife, carefully hollow them out, removing all the seed pulp from the centre.

To make the stuffing, heat the olive oil in a large sauté pan and add the onion, garlic, salt, pepper, allspice and cinnamon. Sauté for 5 minutes, then add the rice and cook for a further 2 minutes, making sure that the rice grains are well coated with the spice mixture.

Add 150ml/¼ pint/⅔ cup water and cook until the rice is al dente: tender with a bite in the centre. Remove from the heat, add the pine nuts, pomegranate seeds and parsley, then leave to cool. Preheat the oven to 180°C/350°F/Gas 4.

Fill the courgette halves with the stuffing and put into an ovenproof dish. Drizzle with a little olive oil and add about 100ml/3½fl oz/scant ½ cup water to the dish.

Bake uncovered for about 30 minutes, basting occasionally with the pan juices. Sprinkle over crumbled feta cheese and serve hot.

DESSERTS, PRESERVES AND DRINKS

SWEET POMEGRANATE SEEDS TASTE SENSATIONAL

WHETHER SPRINKLED OVER A FRESH FRUIT SALAD

OR COMBINED WITH FRESH CREAM FOR A HEADY

DESSERT, AND THE TANGY SYRUP CREATES A

REFRESHING DRINK

FRAGRANT FRUIT AND POMEGRANATE SEED SALAD

The syrup of this exotic fruit salad is flavoured with lime and coffee liqueur. The rich red
pomegranate seeds add extra sweetness as well as colour.

Serves 6
130g/4½oz/½ cup sugar
thinly pared rind and juice of 1
   lime, plus extra fine strips of
   rind, to decorate
150ml/¼ pint/⅔ cup water
60ml/4 tbsp coffee liqueur, such
   as Tia Maria, Kahlúa or
   Toussaint
1 small pineapple, peeled and
   cut into bite-sized chunks
1 papaya, sliced
1 medium mango, cut into
   chunks
seeds of 2 pomegranates
2 passion fruits

Put the sugar and lime rind in a small saucepan with the measured water. Heat gently until the sugar dissolves, then bring to the boil and simmer for 5 minutes. Leave to cool, then strain discarding the lime rind. Stir in the lime juice and liqueur.

Add the pineapple chunks, papaya slices, mango chunks and pomegranate seeds into a bowl. Stir well.

Halve the passion fruits and scoop out the flesh using a teaspoon. Spoon over the salad and serve, decorated with fine strips of lime peel.

Energy 146kcal/620kJ; Protein 1g;
Carbohydrate 33.2g, of which sugars 33.2g;
Fat 0.3g, of which saturates 0g; Cholesterol
0mg; Calcium 40mg; Fibre 2.9g; Sodium
7mg.

SWEET AND SOUR SALAD

This tangy salad is the perfect accompaniment to a variety of spicy dishes and curries, with its clean taste and bright, jewel-like colours of the pomegranate seeds.

Serves 8

1 small cucumber
1 onion, thinly sliced
1 small, ripe pineapple or 425g/
    15oz can pineapple rings
1 green (bell) pepper, seeded
    and thinly sliced
3 firm tomatoes, chopped
30ml/2 tbsp golden granulated
    sugar
45–60ml/3–4 tbsp white wine
    vinegar
120ml/4fl oz/½ cup water
seeds of 1–2 pomegranates
salt

Halve the cucumber lengthways, remove the seeds, slice and spread on a plate with the onion. Sprinkle with salt. After 10 minutes, rinse and dry.

If using a fresh pineapple, peel and core it, removing all the eyes, then cut it into bite-size pieces. If using canned pineapple, drain the rings and cut them into small wedges. Place the pineapple in a bowl with the cucumber, onion, green pepper and tomatoes.

Heat the sugar, vinegar and measured water in a pan, stirring until the sugar has dissolved. Remove the pan from the heat and leave to cool. When cold, add a little salt to taste and pour over the fruit and vegetables. Cover and chill until required. Serve in small bowls, sprinkled with pomegranate seeds.

Energy 38kcal/161kJ; Protein 0.9g; Carbohydrate 8.4g, of which sugars 8.1g; Fat 0.3g, of which saturates 0.1g; Cholesterol 0mg; Calcium 18mg; Fibre 1.5g; Sodium 6mg.

MINTED POMEGRANATE YOGURT WITH GRAPEFRUIT

You can eat this scrumptious yogurt for breakfast or during the day for a healthy snack, but it makes a fabulous dessert served with a delicately scented citrus fruit salad.

Serves 3–4
*300ml / ½ pint / 1¼ cups Greek
    (US strained plain) yogurt*
2–3 pomegranates
*small bunch of mint, finely
    chopped*
*honey or sugar, to taste
    (optional)*

For the grapefruit salad
2 red grapefruit
2 pink grapefruit
1 white grapefruit
*15–30ml / 1–2 tbsp orange
    flower water*
handful of pomegranate seeds
mint leaves

Put the yogurt in a bowl and beat well. Cut open the pomegranates and scoop out the seeds, removing all the bitter pith. Fold the pomegranate seeds and chopped mint into the yogurt. Sweeten with a little honey or sugar, if using, then chill until ready to serve.

Peel the red, pink and white grapefruits, cutting off all the pith. Cut between the membranes to remove the segments, holding the fruit over a bowl to catch the juices.

Discard the membranes and mix the fruit segments with the reserved juices. Sprinkle with the orange flower water and add a little honey or sugar, if using. Add half the pomegranate seeds and stir together gently.

Top the grapefruit salad with the chilled yogurt and add a scattering of pomegranate seeds and mint leaves.

Energy 188kcal/784kJ; Protein 8.8g; Carbohydrate 18g, of which sugars 18g; Fat 10.5g, of which saturates 5.2g; Cholesterol 0mg; Calcium 202mg; Fibre 3.6g; Sodium 82mg.

VARIATION
Alternatively, lime segments work well with the grapefruit and mandarins or tangerines could be used too.

POMEGRANATE AND ORANGE FLOWER WATER CREAMS

Take advantage of fresh pomegranates when in season to make this wonderfully vibrant dessert. The colour will range from pastel pink to vibrant cerise, depending on the type of pomegranates used.

Serves 6

10ml/2 tsp cornflour (cornstarch)
300ml/½ pint/1¼ cups milk
25g/1oz/2 tbsp caster
    (superfine) sugar
3 large pomegranates
30ml/2 tbsp orange flower
    water, plus extra to serve
75ml/5 tbsp grenadine
300ml/½ pint/1¼ cups
    whipping cream

Put the cornflour in a pan and blend to a paste with a little of the milk. Stir in the remaining milk and the sugar and cook, stirring constantly, until the mixture thickens. Pour it into a bowl, cover the surface closely with baking parchment and leave to cool.

Cut 2 of the pomegranates in half and squeeze out the juice, using a lemon squeezer. Add the juice to the cornflour mixture, with the orange flower water, grenadine and cream. Stir lightly to mix.

By hand: Stir to mix, then pour into a container and freeze for 3–4 hours, beating twice as it thickens.

Using an ice cream maker: Churn the mixture until it is thick enough to hold its shape.

Spoon the ice cream into one large, or six individual freezerproof serving dishes and freeze for at least 2 hours, or overnight.

Transfer the creams to the refrigerator 30 minutes before serving. Remove the seeds from the remaining pomegranate and toss in the extra orange flower water before sprinkling over each cream.

VARIATION

To accentuate the flavour of this dessert, the seeds from 12 cardamom pods can be added with the orange flower water.

Energy 278kcal/1151kJ; Protein 2.8g;
Carbohydrate 10.6g, of which sugars 9.1g;
Fat 22.1g, of which saturates 13.9g;
Cholesterol 60mg; Calcium 101mg; Fibre
0.6g; Sodium 36mg.

WHEAT IN FRAGRANT HONEY WITH POMEGRANATE SEEDS

In Lebanon, this nourishing dessert is traditionally prepared with young green wheat or barley and decorated with almonds and pomegranate seeds to mark significant events.

Serves 6

225g/8oz/1¼ cups whole wheat grains, soaked overnight and drained
1 litre/1¾ pints/4 cups water
60–90ml/4–6 tbsp fragrant runny honey
30ml/2 tbsp orange flower water
30ml/2 tbsp rose water
30–45ml/2–3 tbsp raisins or sultanas (golden raisins), soaked in warm water for 30 minutes and drained
30ml/2 tbsp pine nuts, soaked in water for 2 hours
30ml/2 tbsp blanched almonds, soaked in water for 2 hours
seeds of 1 pomegranate

Place the soaked whole wheat grains in a heavy pan with the water and bring to the boil.

Reduce the heat, cover, and simmer for 1 hour, until the wheat is tender, and most of the water is absorbed.

Meanwhile, heat the honey and stir in the orange flower and rose waters – don't let the mixture boil. Stir in the raisins or sultanas and turn off the heat.

Transfer the wheat grains to a serving bowl, or individual bowls, and pour the honey and raisins over the top.

Sprinkle over the nuts and pomegranate seeds and serve while still warm, or leave to cool and chill in the refrigerator before serving.

COOK'S TIP
You could also try serving this for breakfast or as part of a brunch.

Energy 193kcal/806kJ; Protein 4.1g; Carbohydrate 30.9g, of which sugars 11.5g; Fat 6.6g, of which saturates 0.5g; Cholesterol 0mg; Calcium 23mg; Fibre 0.6g; Sodium 3mg.

POMEGRANATE SALAD WITH PINE NUTS AND HONEY

This pretty, decorative fruit salad can be served as a refreshing dish between courses and as an accompaniment to other sweet dishes, as well as a traditional dessert at the end of a meal.

Serves 4–6
45–60ml/3–4 tbsp pine nuts
3 pomegranates
30ml/2 tbsp orange flower
    water
15–30ml/1–2 tbsp fragrant
    runny honey
handful of small mint leaves, to
    decorate

Place the pine nuts in a bowl, cover with the water and leave for approximately 2 hours.

Cut the pomegranates into quarters, transferring any excess juice to a bowl.

Extract the seeds, taking care to discard the bitter white pith and membrane, and place in a bowl with the juice. Drain the pine nuts and add them to the bowl.

Stir in the orange flower water and honey, cover the bowl, and chill in the refrigerator.

Serve the salad chilled, or at room temperature, decorated with a few mint leaves.

Energy 82kcal/344kJ; Protein 1.3g; Carbohydrate 8.2g, of which sugars 8.1g; Fat 5.2g, of which saturates 0.4g; Cholesterol 0mg; Calcium 4mg; Fibre 1.2g; Sodium 2mg.

CARAMELIZED PINEAPPLE IN POMEGRANATE SYRUP

This stunning dessert, garnished with bright pomegranate seeds, is superb for entertaining. The tangy, zesty flavours of lemon grass and mint bring out the exquisite sweetness of the pineapple.

Serves 4

30ml/2 tbsp very finely chopped lemon grass, and 2 lemon grass stalks, halved lengthways
350g/12oz/1¾ cups caster (superfine) sugar
10ml/2 tsp chopped fresh mint leaves
2 small, ripe pineapples (approximately 600g/1lb 5oz each)
15ml/1 tbsp sunflower oil
60ml/4 tbsp pomegranate seeds
crème fraîche, to serve

Place all of the lemon grass, 250g/9oz of the sugar and the mint leaves in a non-stick wok. Pour over 150ml/¼ pint/⅔ cup of water and place over a medium heat and bring to the boil.

Reduce the heat under the wok and simmer the mixture for 10–15 minutes, until thickened. Strain into a glass bowl, reserving the halved lemon grass stalks, then set aside.

Using a sharp knife, peel and core the pineapples and cut into 1cm/½in-thick slices, then sprinkle the slices with the remaining sugar.

Brush a large non-stick wok with the oil and place over a medium heat. Working in batches, cook the sugared pineapple slices for 4–5 minutes, on each side, until lightly caramelized.

Transfer the pineapple slices to a flat serving dish and scatter over the pomegranate seeds.

Pour the lemon grass syrup over the fruit and garnish with the reserved stalks. Serve with crème fraîche.

Energy 493kcal/2101kJ; Protein 1.6g;
Carbohydrate 121.7g, of which sugars
121.7g; Fat 3.4g, of which saturates 0.3g;
Cholesterol 0mg; Calcium 101mg; Fibre
3.6g; Sodium 11mg.

POMEGRANATE JEWELLED CHEESECAKE

This light cheesecake is flavoured with coconut and has a stunning pomegranate glaze. For the best results, make the biscuit crumbs as finely as possible.

Serves 8

225g/8oz oat biscuits (cookies)
75g/3oz/⅓ cup unsalted
*   butter, melted*

For the filling

45ml/3 tbsp orange juice
15ml/1 tbsp powdered gelatine
250g/9oz/generous 1 cup
*   mascarpone*
200g/7oz/scant 1 cup full-fat
*   soft cheese*
75g/3oz/¾ cup icing
*   (confectioners') sugar, sifted*
200ml/7fl oz/scant 1 cup
*   coconut cream*
2 egg whites

For the topping

seeds of 2 pomegranates
grated rind and juice of 1 orange
30ml/2 tbsp sugar
15ml/1 tbsp arrowroot, mixed
*   to a paste with 30ml/2 tbsp*
*   Kirsch*
a few drops of red food
*   colouring (optional)*

Grease a 23cm/9in springform cake tin (pan). Crumb the biscuits in a food processor or blender. Add the melted butter and process briefly to combine. Spoon into the prepared tin, press the mixture in well, then chill while you make the filling.

For the filling, pour the orange juice into a heatproof bowl, sprinkle the gelatine on top and set aside for 5 minutes until spongy. Place the bowl in a pan of hot water and stir until the gelatine has dissolved.

In a bowl, beat together both cheeses and the icing sugar, then gradually beat in the coconut cream. Whisk the egg whites in a grease-free bowl to soft peaks. Quickly stir the melted gelatine into the coconut mixture and fold in the egg whites. Pour over the biscuit base, level and chill until set.

For the cheesecake topping, place the pomegranate seeds in a pan and add the orange rind and juice and sugar. Bring to the boil, then lower the heat, cover and simmer for 5 minutes. Add the arrowroot paste and heat, stirring constantly, until thickened. Stir in the food colouring, if using. Allow to cool, stirring occasionally.

Pour the glaze over the top of the set cheesecake, then chill. To serve, run a knife between the edge of the tin and the cheesecake, then remove the side of the tin.

Energy 590kcal/2461kJ; Protein 8g; Carbohydrate 45g, of which sugars 22g; Fat 43g, of which saturates 29g; Cholesterol 86mg; Calcium 86mg; Fibre 1g; Sodium 372mg.

ALMOND AND ORANGE CAKE

This is a modern variation on a classic almond cake. The pomegranate and honey syrup is poured onto the cake after baking to ensure a wonderfully moist texture.

Serves 10

150g/5oz/10 tbsp butter, cubed, plus extra for greasing
1 large navel orange, unpeeled
350g/12oz/3 cups ground almonds
300g/11oz/generous 1½ cups caster (superfine) sugar
115g/4oz/1 cup plain (all-purpose) flour
5ml/1 tsp baking powder
6 eggs
seeds of 2 pomegranates

For the syrup

250ml/8fl oz/1 cup pomegranate juice
60ml/4 tbsp clear honey
15ml/1 tbsp pomegranate molasses

Grease a 15cm/6in square baking tin (pan) with butter, and line with baking parchment.

Put all the ingredients for the syrup in a pan and stir well over medium heat until the honey has dissolved. Cook, stirring, for 10–12 minutes, or until the liquid has a syrupy consistency.

Put the whole orange in a small pan, cover with water and boil for 25 minutes, or until the skin is soft. Remove and cool. Put the whole orange in a food processor or blender and process to a purée. Set aside.

Preheat the oven to 180°C/350°F/ Gas 4. Put the ground almonds into a mixing bowl and add half the sugar, the flour and the baking powder. Mix well.

Beat the remaining sugar with the butter cubes until light and creamy. Add the eggs one at a time, beating well after each addition. Add the puréed orange and mix well.

Gradually fold in the almond mixture and pour this into the prepared baking tin. Bake for 50–60 minutes. Test to see if it's fully cooked by inserting a skewer; the cake is ready if the skewer comes out clean. When cooked, remove from the oven and leave to cool slightly before turning it out on to a rack to cool completely.

Using a skewer, make deep holes in the top of the cake and slowly pour over the syrup, which will soak into the cake. Pile the pomegranate seeds on top, and serve.

Energy 569kcal/2381kJ; Protein 13g; Carbohydrate 53.5g, of which sugars 41.1g; Fat 35.4g, of which saturates 10.7g; Cholesterol 149mg; Calcium 148mg; Fibre 3.3g; Sodium 163mg.

POMEGRANATE AND GRENADINE JELLY

The slightly tart flavoured, red flesh of the pomegranate makes the most wonderful jelly. Be careful though, because pomegranate juice can stain indelibly when spilt on clothing.

Makes about 900g/2lb
seeds of 6 pomegranates
120ml/4fl oz/½ cup grenadine syrup
juice and pips (seeds) of 2 oranges
300ml/½ pint/1¼ cups water
about 900g/2lb/4½ cups preserving or granulated sugar, warmed

Put the pomegranate seeds in a large, clean bowl and crush to release their juice. Transfer them to a pan and add the grenadine, orange juice, pips and water.

Bring the mixture to the boil, cover and simmer for 1½ hours. Mash the fruit and leave to cool slightly, then pour into a scalded jelly bag suspended over a bowl and leave to drain overnight.

Measure the juice into a pan and add 450g/1lb/2¼ cups sugar for every 600ml/1 pint/2½ cups juice.

Heat, stirring, over a low heat until the sugar has dissolved. Increase the heat and boil rapidly, without stirring, for 5–10 minutes, or until the jelly reaches setting point (105°C/220°F).

Remove the pan from the heat and skim off any scum. Ladle into warmed sterilized jars, cover, seal and label. Store in a cool place and consume within 18 months.

Energy 3776kcal/16,114kJ; Protein 5.5g; Carbohydrate 1000.5g, of which sugars 1000.5g; Fat 0.2g, of which saturates 0g; Cholesterol 0mg; Calcium 511mg; Fibre 0.8g; Sodium 76mg.

PEAR AND POMEGRANATE JELLY

This delicate jelly has a faintly exotic perfume. Pears are not naturally rich in pectin so liquid pectin needs to be added to the jelly during cooking to help it achieve a good set.

Makes about 1.2kg/2½lb
900g/2lb pears
pared rind and juice of 2 lemons
1 cinnamon stick
750ml/1¼ pints/3 cups water
900g/2lb pomegranates
about 900g/2lb/4½ cups
 preserving or granulated
 sugar
250ml/8fl oz/1 cup liquid pectin
15ml/1 tbsp rose water
 (optional)

Wash and remove the stalks from the pears and chop the fruit roughly. Put the chopped fruit in a large heavy pan with the lemon rind and juice, cinnamon stick and measured water.

Bring the mixture to the boil, then reduce the heat to low, cover with a lid and simmer gently for about 15 minutes.

Remove the lid from the pan, stir the fruit mixture, then leave to simmer, uncovered, for a further 15 minutes.

While the pears are simmering, cut the pomegranates in half horizontally, and use a lemon squeezer to extract all the juice: there should be about 250ml/8fl oz/1 cup.

Add the pomegranate juice to the pan and bring back to the boil. Reduce the heat and simmer for 2 minutes. Pour the fruit and juices into a sterilized jelly bag suspended over a large bowl. Leave to drip for at least 3 hours.

Measure the strained juice into the cleaned pan, adding 450g/1lb/ 2¼ cups sugar for every 600ml/1 pint/2½ cups juice.

Heat gently, stirring occasionally, until the sugar has dissolved. Bring to the boil, then boil rapidly for 3 minutes. Remove the pan from the heat and stir in the liquid pectin.

Skim any scum from the surface, then stir in the rose water, if using. Pour the jelly into warmed sterilized jars. Cover and seal. Store in a cool, dark place and use within 18 months.

Energy 3756kcal/16,022kJ; Protein 6g; Carbohydrate 993.6g, of which sugars 993.6g; Fat 0.4g, of which saturates 0g; Cholesterol 0mg; Calcium 529mg; Fibre 7.7g; Sodium 66mg.

COOK'S TIP
Once opened, store the jelly in the refrigerator and use within 3 months.

POMEGRANATE JUICE PLUS

Pomegranate juice has an exotic and distinctive flavour and makes a delicious base for this treat of a juice, which is mildly spiced with a hint of fresh ginger.

Makes 2 glasses

2 pomegranates
4 fresh figs
15g/½oz fresh root ginger, peeled
10ml/2 tsp lime juice
ice cubes and lime wedges, to serve

COOK'S TIP
Pomegranates with a rich reddish skin is usually a sign that the seeds inside will be vibrant and sweet.

Halve the pomegranates. Working over a bowl to catch the juices, pull away the skin to remove the jewel-like clusters of seeds.

Quarter the figs and roughly chop the ginger. Push the figs and ginger through a juicer. Push the pomegranate seeds through, reserving a few for decoration. Stir in the lime juice. Pour over ice cubes and lime wedges, then serve.

SPICED POMEGRANATE AND PEAR FIZZ

Pears make a good partner for the fresh tang of pomegranates. Juice the fruits in advance if you have the time, so the spice can mellow into the fruits, all ready for topping up with fizzy tonic water.

Makes 2 glasses

2 pears
1.5ml/¼ tsp ground allspice
1 pomegranate
5–10ml/1–2 tsp clear honey
ice cubes
tonic water
*pear wedges and pomegranate
seeds, to decorate*

Using a small, sharp knife, chop the pears into large chunks. Mix the allspice in a jug or pitcher with 15ml/1 tbsp boiling water.

Halve the pomegranate. Working over the jug to catch the juices, peel away the skin and layers of pith to leave the clusters of seeds.

Push the pears and pomegranate seeds through a juicer and mix together in the jug with the allspice. Stir in a little honey to sweeten, then chill.

Pour the juice into glasses until two-thirds full. Serve with ice cubes, pear wedges and pomegranate seeds. Top up with tonic water.

COOK'S TIP
Ideal for slimmers, pears are virtually fat-free and contain absolutely no cholesterol or sodium. They also provide significant amounts of vitamin C and potassium.

INDEX

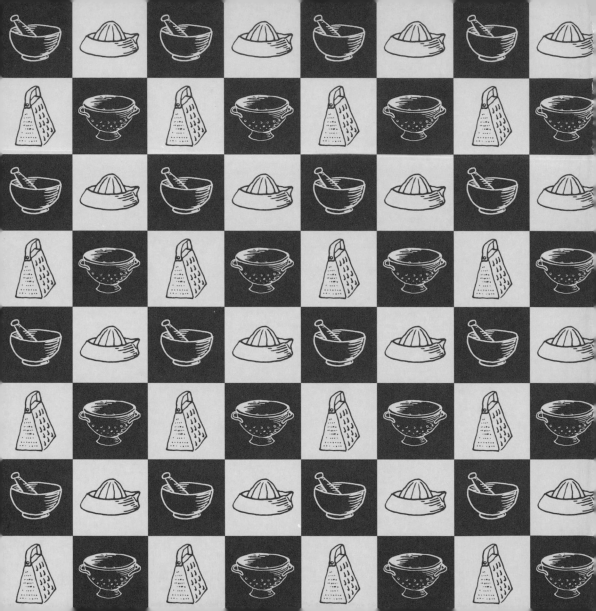